D1252426

EXTREME NATURE

HARSH HABITATS

Anita Ganeri

Raintree

Chicago, Illinois

www.capstonepub.com
Visit our website to find out more information about Heinemann-Raintree books.

To order:
☎ Phone 800-747-4992
💻 Visit www.capstonepub.com to browse our catalog and order online.

Edited by Dan Nunn, Rebecca Rissman, and Catherine Veitch
Designed by Cynthia Della-Rovere
Picture research by Tracy Cummins
Production by Alison Parsons

Originated by Capstone Global Library
Printed and bound in China by CTPS

16 15 14 13 12
10 9 8 7 6 5 4 3 2 1

Library of Congress Cataloging-in-Publication Data
Ganeri, Anita
Harsh habitats / Anita Ganeri.
p. cm.—(Extreme nature)
Includes bibliographical references and index.
ISBN 978-1-4109-4697-3 (hb)—ISBN 978-1-4109-4702-4 (pb) 1. Adaptation (Biology)—Juvenile literature. 2. Extreme environments—Juvenile literature. I. Title.
QH546.G36 2013
578.4—dc23   2011038391

Acknowledgments
We would like to thank the following for permission to reproduce photographs: Corbis p. 27 (© Michael Durham/Visuals Unlimited); FLPA p. 21 (Konrad Wothe/Minden Pictures); Getty Images pp. 7 (Arctic-Images), 10 (Karen Gowlett-Holmes), 24 (Stephen Alvarez); istockphoto p. 14 (12924648); National Geographic Stock pp. 11, 12, 18 (NORBERT WU/MINDEN PICTURES); Photolibrary pp. 6 (Juan Carlos Munoz/age footstock), 9 (Superstock), 13 (Marevision Marevision), 19 (Steven Kazlowski), 26 (Crispin Hughes); Shutterstock pp. 4 (© Petrova Maria), 5 (© Zacarias Pereira da Mata), 8 (© 2009fotofriends), 15 (© Dmitry Savinov), 16 (© Witold Kaszkin), 17 (© Jan Martin Will), 20 (© Galyna Andrushko), 22 (© Patrick Poendl), 23 (© Alexander Yu. Zotov), 25 (© Ivan Kuzmin).

Cover photograph of Namib Desert reproduced with permission of Shutterstock (© Pichugin Dmitry). Background photograph of the cracked earth reproduced with permission of Shutterstock (© vadim kozlovsky).

Every effort has been made to contact copyright holders of material reproduced in this book. Any omissions will be rectified in subsequent printings if notice is given to the publisher.

Disclaimer
All the Internet addresses (URLs) given in this book were valid at the time of going to press. However, due to the dynamic nature of the Internet, some addresses may have changed, or sites may have changed or ceased to exist since publication. While the author and publisher regret any inconvenience this may cause readers, no responsibility for any such changes can be accepted by either the author or the publisher.

Some words are shown in bold, **like this**. You can find out what they mean by looking in the glossary.

Contents

What Are Harsh Habitats?

Did you know that animals and plants live in some of the hottest, coldest, highest, and wettest places on Earth? The places where plants and animals live are called habitats.

DID YOU KNOW?
Plants and animals living in harsh habitats need special **features** to **survive**.

Mighty Mountains

High up on a mountain, it is very cold, with **gale-force** winds. The slopes may be bare and rocky, or they may be covered with ice and snow. So how do mountain plants and animals **survive**?

Vicuñas live in the Andes Mountains, in South America. They have thick coats to keep them warm.

Mountain goats are excellent climbers. Their **hooves** have sharp edges for gripping onto rocks. They also have pads that stop them from slipping.

Elfin trees grow very low to the ground.
This keeps them out of the wind.

Deep, Dark Seas

Deep down in the sea, it is pitch black and cold. Many deep-sea fish make their own lights. The lights are made of billions of tiny, glowing **bacteria**.

The anglerfish's light helps it to spot **prey**.

Flashlight fish have lights under their eyes. They can turn their lights off by covering them with skin. This helps them to escape from enemies.

light

gulper eel

Gulper eels live deep in the Atlantic Ocean. They have huge mouths for gulping down any food they can find.

This snailfish is found deep in the ocean.

Steamy Rain Forests

Tropical rain forests are always hot and wet. They can be dangerous places to live in. Many animals have tricks for staying safe. Poison dart frogs have brightly colored skin to warn hungry birds that they are **poisonous**.

DID YOU KNOW?
Poison dart frogs get their name because people have used their poison to create poisoned darts.

Freezing Cold Poles

The Arctic (North Pole) and Antarctica (South Pole) are the coldest and iciest places on the planet. In winter, the temperature in the Arctic can fall below -31°F!

Polar bears live in the Arctic. They have thick, oily fur with a thick layer of fat underneath. This keeps them warm and dry.

ice fish

The seas around the North and South Poles are cold and icy. Ice fish in Antarctica have a special chemical in their blood that stops their bodies from freezing.

Weddell seals use their large teeth to gnaw, or chew, breathing holes in the ice.

Deadly Deserts

Deserts can be baking hot in the daytime. Many desert animals spend the day in cool **burrows** underground.

DID YOU KNOW?
The temperature in the Sahara Desert can reach 113°F in the day.

Fennec foxes in the Sahara Desert in Africa have huge ears. Their ears give off heat, which helps the foxes to keep cool.

Deserts are very dry places. It is difficult for animals and plants to find water. Camels store water in their bodies. They can go for days without drinking.

DID YOU KNOW?
In parts of the Atacama Desert, in Chile, it has not rained for hundreds of years.

23

Going Underground

Caves are underground spaces. They form when rain and river water carve the rocks away. Caves are usually dark and damp.

DID YOU KNOW?
Some cave fish cannot see. They do not need to see in the dark caves.

Caves make good **roosting** places for animals such as bats. Bats cling upside down on the cave walls.

Concrete Jungle

A busy, noisy city can be a harsh habitat. But many animals, such as foxes, raccoons, and coyotes, have moved into cities. This is because their wild homes are under threat.

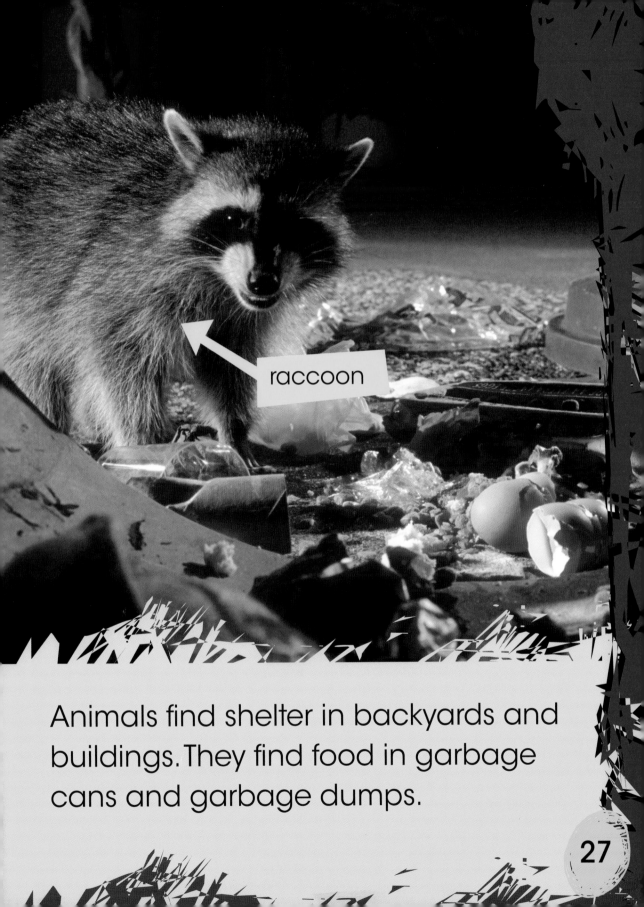

raccoon

Animals find shelter in backyards and buildings. They find food in garbage cans and garbage dumps.

Quiz: What Am I?

Read the clues, then try to figure out "What am I?" Find the answers at the bottom of page 29. But guess first!

1) I live on a mountain.
I have sharp **hooves**.
I am good at climbing.
What am I?

2) I have a big mouth.
I am a type of eel.
I live in the deep sea.
What am I?

3) I am **poisonous**.
I live in the rain forest.
I have brightly colored skin.
What am I?

4) I have thick, white fur.
I live in the Arctic.
I have thick fat under my skin.
What am I?

5) I am a type of fox.
I have big ears.
I live in the desert.
What am I?

Glossary

bacteria tiny living things

burrow hole that an animal digs in the ground

feature special body part, pattern, or type of behavior

gale-force describes a very strong wind found in a storm or high in the mountains

hooves hard coverings on a goat or horse's feet

poisonous containing a substance that can harm or kill

prey animal that is hunted for food

roost rest or sleep on a perch, such as a tree branch or cave wall

survive stay alive

tropical rain forest forest that is warm and wet all year round

Find Out More

Books

Cooper, Sharon Katz. *Horrible Habitats* series. Chicago: Raintree, 2010.

Piper, Ross. *Surviving in the World's Most Extreme Places* (Fact Finders). Mankato, Minn.: Capstone, 2010.

Pyers, Greg, and Mary Quigley. *Habitat Explorer* series. Chicago: Raintree, 2005.

Websites

environment.nationalgeographic.com/ environment/habitats/?source=NavEnvHab

This National Geographic Website covers a range of habitats.

wwf.panda.org/about_our_earth/ ecoregions/about/habitat_types/habitats/

This WWF Website describes animal life in a variety of habitats.